CUSTOMS & ETIQUETTE OF
KOREA

ABOUT THE AUTHORS

JAMES HOARE and SUSAN PARES are husband and wife, who both worked in Korea. They lived in Seoul from 1981 to 1985, and have made frequent visits there. Their last joint publication was *Beijing* published by ABC-CLIO World Bibliographical Series Vol. 226. (2000)

ILLUSTRATED BY
IN-SOO PAICK & IRENE SANDERSON

CUSTOMS & ETIQUETTE OF
KOREA

James Hoare &
Susan Pares

Customs & Etiquette of Korea
by James Hoare & Susan Pares

First published 1996 by Global Books Ltd.
Second edition 2000
This edition published 2005 by
Simple Guides an imprint of Bravo Ltd.
59 Hutton Grove
London N12 8DS
Tel: +44 (0) 208 446 2440
Fax: +44 (0) 208 446 2441
Enquiries: office@kuperard.co.uk
www.kuperard.co.uk

ISBN-13: 978-1-85733-395-4
ISBN-10: 1-85733-395-0

British Library Cataloguing in Publication Data
A CIP catalogue entry for this book
is available from the British Library

Cover image: ©Patrick Wass / www.travel-ink.co.uk
Set in Futura 11 on 12 pt by Bookman, Hayes
Printed and bound in China

Contents

Introducing Korea
'Land of the Morning Calm'

In front of the South Gate, Seoul

The Korean peninsula curves out of the land mass of Northeast Asia, dividing the Yellow Sea from what the Koreans call the East Sea, which often appears on Western maps as the Sea of Japan. To the north, there is a long land border with China, and a short one with Russia. The peninsula is rugged, with Mount Paektu on the Sino-Korean border reaching a height of 2,744 metres, and is spectacularly beautiful in places. The climate is varied: semi-tropical in the southern island of Cheju, but in the rest of the peninsula varying from sub-zero winter temperatures to summer monsoons.

Koreans trace their historical origins back to the Neolithic age (c.5000–1000BC), when the mythical founder of the Korean state, the half-human, half-divine Tangun, is supposed to have flourished, but it is only much later, well after the beginning of the Christian era, that the first recognizable states emerge. One of these, Silla, succeeded in uniting most of the peninsula in 668 AD, thus helping to create a sense of separate identity among the 'Korean peoples' from the Chinese to the north.

BUDDHISM FLOURISHES

It was during this period that Buddhism, introduced from China, flourished among the Korean peoples. Silla was succeeded by the Koryo kingdom (918–1392 AD), from which, through China, the West learnt the name 'Korea'. During this period, Korea made many advances in military science, particularly in the use of rockets and other explosives, and also began the development of printing. Raids by Chinese bandits and Japanese pirates in the late fourteenth century increased the importance of the country's military élite. One general, Yi Song-gye, staged a coup d'état in 1392 and proclaimed himself king of a new Choson dynasty.

The Choson or Yi dynasty went on to rule Korea for the next 500 years or so – until the

Japanese occupied the country in 1910. The capital was moved from Kaesong to Hanyang (modern Seoul), which became, and has remained, the economic, social and political centre of the country. Under the Yi, Buddhism fell from favour, to be replaced by Confucianism, also imported from China. This new philosophy, with its strong emphasis on social order and education, came to dominate most aspects of Korean life, and its influence can still be traced today.

Buddhism did not disappear, but the monks, forced out of the cities, moved to remote mountain areas. Even today, most of South Korea's major Buddhist temples are to be found in hills and remote valleys, though the expansion of the cities has brought others back into urban areas.

Unrest among Korea's neighbours, China and Japan, brought problems for Korea. A Japanese attempt to use the peninsula as a path to China turned into the long-drawn out *Imjin* war, from 1592 to 1598, which left Korea devasted. Many monasteries and palaces were destroyed at this time; some remained in ruins until the twentieth century, a constant reminder of Japan's aggression. Korea also suffered as the Manchu seized control of China and its dependencies in the 1630s and 1640s.

It was hardly surprising, therefore, that Korea tended to turn in upon itself from the seventeenth century onwards. Some formal contacts, which often masked trade relations, were maintained with both China and Japan, and through China,

Koreans learnt of Roman Catholicism. Some converted, only to be heavily persecuted. In general, however, Koreans sought to be left alone.

JAPAN ANNEXES KOREA

The country was thus poorly placed to resist Western and Japanese pressure to open up to foreign trade and residence in the latter years of the nineteenth century. Two wars, the Sino-Japanese War of 1894-95 and the Russo-Japanese War of 1904-05, were fought over the issue of which country should control Korea. Japan won both. Other foreign powers showed little interest in the peninsula after 1905, when Japan proclaimed a protectorate over Korea. This was followed by outright annexation in 1910.

For the next thirty-five years Korea suffered harsh colonial rule until the end of the Second World War brought liberation in 1945. All development in the Korean peninsula under the Japanese was subordinate to the needs of Japan, a trend which grew worse as Japan moved onto an all-out war footing after 1937. This also led to an intensification of the Japanese campaign to assimilate Koreans into the Japanese Empire. Teaching of the Korean language was forbidden, and Koreans were compelled to take Japanese names.

Korean hopes for the restoration of a unified independent state were not realized. The peninsula was divided into Soviet and American zones, which led to the emergence of two separate states in 1948, the Democratic People's Republic of Korea (North Korea) and the Republic of Korea (South Korea). North Korea's attempt at unification by force in 1950 only succeeded in perpetuating the division, which lasts until today.

In the West, Korea became known in the nineteenth century as the 'Land of the Morning Calm' – a mistranslation of '*Choson*', which means 'morning freshness' – or the 'Hermit Kingdom'. However true these titles were originally, they have little validity today. The title 'Hermit Kingdom' might still apply to North Korea, which has had relatively few contacts in the West. It can certainly no longer be applied to the Republic of Korea, a dynamic and fast-growing state, which is known worldwide for its high rate of economic growth and as the host country for both the 1986 Asian Games and the 1988 Olympic Games.

ECONOMIC RECOVERY

The economic crisis that hit several Asian states, including South Korea, in 1997 seems to have been a temporary setback; by January 2000, South Korean economic growth had rebounded to 10% per annum. Some problems remained, but the worst of the crisis appeared to be over. The 2000 Asian Games, to be held in the port city of Pusan, and the 2002 World Cup, which will be jointly hosted with Japan, should help to boost South Korean confidence.

The rapid changes that have affected the Korean peninsula over the last 100 years have left their mark. War and bitter experience as a colony of Japan from 1910 to 1945, followed by post-war division and the fratricidal strife of the Korean War (1950–53), have given way in South Korea to economic and social development. While this has in turn had its cost, modern Korea has survived with much that is traditional still intact. In both North and South Korea visitors will find a country where old and new mingle on all sides. They will find also a heady mixture of passion and consideration, fervour and politeness.

What will strike most visitors, however, are the grandeur of Korea's scenery, the exhilaration of its cities and the friendliness of its people. This 'briefing' book aims to provide a guide for the visitor through the maze of Korean customs and etiquette so that visiting Korea is made simpler and more enjoyable. Most of what follows relates to South Korea. Chapter 9 offers some general guidelines and tentative pointers for the visitor to North Korea, now opening up a little to tourism as the first steps towards reconciliation are taken by the two governments.

Special thanks are due to Yeon Jae-hoon, Larry Ross, James Grayson, Ian Soutar and Mike Reilly who read and commented on the first version of the text. Stephen Brown, British ambassador in Seoul from 1997 to 2000, unwittingly provided the opportunity to revise and update the original text. A visit to North Korea in May 1998 provided one of the authors with a unique perspective on developments in the northern half of the peninsula. Views expressed and errors committed remain the responsibility of the authors.

JAMES HOARE
SUSAN PARES

Map of Korea

CHINA

Ch'ongjin

Kilchu

Sinuiju

Hamhung

Anju
Hungnam

Yonghung
NORTH
KOREA

Wonsan
Sea of Japan
(East Sea)

P'yongyang

Sariwon

Haeju
Kaesong
DEMILITARIZED ZONE

Kangnung

Seoul
Inch'on
Songnam
Samchok
Suwon

Ch'ungju

Ch'ongju

Yellow Sea
Andong
SOUTH
KOREA

Taejon

Kunsan
Taegu

Chonju
Ulsan

Kwangju
Masan
Chinju
Pusan

Mokp'o

Korea Strait

Cheju

Land over 1000 metres

0   200km

1

Social Relations & the Visitor

Hanbok – Korean costume

To the Chinese, Korea was 'the country of courteous people in the East'. This reflected the Koreans' traditional esteem for decorum, courtesy and propriety, derived from the teachings of Confucius. Even today, Korean hospitality is memorable.

At the same time, Koreans do not favour demonstrative behaviour in front of those they do not know well. They tend to be remote and apparently stand-offish in the presence of strangers. They are not friendly to people they meet on the street, whether Koreans or foreigners. In particular, they do not feel obliged to greet in friendly fashion those to whom they have not been introduced. This is perhaps more obvious in big cities such as Seoul or Pusan, which are just as impersonal as cities in the West.

It is a fact that strangers will push and shove in a way that would be unthinkable in Western cities or in Japan. In this, the foreign visitor is likely to be treated just like a Korean. Nevertheless, if you are invited to visit a Korean family, you will be given quite a different reception. At home, or in his/her place of work, a Korean will be most courteous and polite to visitors.

Hot Tip: Common Interests = Close Relationships

Koreans can quickly strike up close relationships when they find that they share something in common with a new acquaintance.

Among a group of Koreans, especially those meeting for the first time, great efforts will be made to establish links in common. These can be family, school or university ties, home towns shared, or even hobbies. The sense of belonging to a group, of being 'one of us', is very important to Koreans and plays a major role in developing human relations. It can also exclude outsiders quite pointedly.

Yet it is possible to get around the problem. As a foreigner, you will not share family or home town links, but may have hobbies in common, or possibly have attended the same university as your Korean host did when studying in your country. This will provide a useful talking point and bond.

It is very likely that you will be asked a number of personal questions about your age, your education, your religion, your marital status – very few Koreans remain unmarried – and the composition of your family. This is not 'nosiness', or a wish to satisfy idle curiosity, but an attempt to learn important information that will allow your Korean acquaintances to position themselves in relation to you: to be older, married (with children), or to hold a senior position in your company, or a doctorate, for example, all give important social standing.

Hot Tip: Please Meet 'Our' Wife!

Koreans frequently use 'we' when it is more natural in English to say 'I'. They prefer to say 'our country' instead of 'my country' and 'our house' instead of 'my house'. You might even hear 'our wife' instead of 'my wife'! Do not worry. This, too, is part of the Korean – and indeed wider East Asian – emphasis on the group rather than the individual.

At first sight, some South Koreans appear very Westernized. The style of life, especially in the cities, is similar to that in other big cities throughout the world. War and development have left few ancient buildings. Some modern Korean architecture draws on traditional styles but most is fairly nondescript. You can eat in McDonald's or Wendy's. Planet Hollywood has arrived in Seoul, as has the Hard Rock Cafe. In addition, there are many Western-style restaurants and shops, run by Koreans, which show the Korean desire to be modern and international. Korean men and women wear Western-style clothes on most occasions.

Just occasionally, a Korean man will appear in traditional costume, *hanbok*, especially at New Year. A few wear it at home and it remains popular among some older men who may don it for a Saturday or Sunday outing to the park. On the other hand, Korean women wear traditional dress more frequently; it is very becoming and often quite gorgeous. You will often see *hanbok* at weddings and the accompanying photographic sessions in big hotels, traditional restaurants and at cultural events, but it is steadily disappearing from every-day life.

MEN & WOMEN

Yet some aspects of traditional Korea do survive. There is widespread respect for those who are older. This is another inheritance from Confucianism, which is still a strong cultural influence in Korea. To show respect to the elderly and to those senior in years is highly regarded. It is therefore not advisable to sit until those more senior have taken their seats, and it also makes a good impression if you stand up when somebody more senior enters the room. You may find that Korean young people are reluctant to eat, drink alcohol or smoke in front of parents or teachers. If you are young, or even just young-looking, do not be offended if an older Korean abandons you in mid-conversation to talk to an older colleague.

'. . . holding the bags of standing passengers'

In theory, at least, this respect for seniority extends to those one meets travelling on buses, trains and the subway. In practice, however, the anonymity described above often takes over, and it is becoming less common for somebody to offer a seat to an elderly person.

Hot Tip: No Weight-lifting Here!

One vestige of the past you may still find in use is for those seated to hold the bags of standing passengers. Do not be surprised, therefore, if a heavy bag is quietly taken from you on buses and trains; it is not a thief but a seated passenger wanting to relieve you of a burden for a few stops.

Confucius emphasized respect for the elderly, but he meant elderly men. Neither women nor children ranked very high in his system of priorities. In the past, a woman was taught that in youth she should be obedient to her parents; when married obedient to her husband; and in old age obedient to her son.

Traditional Korean house and dress

Much of this has now changed. Korean women will smoke and drink, lead independent lives and petition for divorce. A growing number manage their own businesses. Women are well represented in some professions. As in other countries, many are engaged in teaching, and there are several female paediatricians. In the next few years, they are to be admitted to the military academies for officer training. There is a strong feminist movement in South Korea, with departments specializing in women's studies at several universities. A number of women have entered politics, and a few have become ministers.

Yet the idea of male superiority and female subordination has not entirely disappeared. A middle-class Korean man will boast that he is a 'tiger' at home, even if he does hand all his wages over to his wife at the end of the month, receiving pocket-money in return. Korean women, therefore, are not necessarily used to the courtesies shown to women in the West. They will be pleased if a foreigner holds open a door for them or allows them to go first out of a lift (elevator), though they may also be a little embarrassed at the courtesy and unwilling to accept it at first.

Conversely, a Western woman in Korea may find that she is not treated as she would be at home, even if she is conducting business in her own right. Usually the courtesy extended to a visitor will ensure that she is well received during ordinary business transactions. She will be invited to lunch or dinner, especially if this is in a Western restaurant. But she is unlikely to be included in post-work entertainment, particularly if this is to include a late night drinking session.

2

Business & Social Life

Koreans tend to dress formally during the work-ing week. This applies to both men and women. Men will generally wear sombre-coloured Western suits. There are some exceptions. Among academics, for instance, it is not unusual to find sports jackets, though usually of a fairly conserva-tive style and colour. An artist may wear a French-style beret, and have a beard. In some of the bigger Korean companies, all staff, whether managerial or shop-floor workers, will wear the company uniform.

During the hottest period in summer, some of this formality may be relaxed, and open-necked shirts become the norm in government offices. If in doubt, however, a man should wear a tie.

Hot Tip: Dress Conservatively

Women will find that their Korean counterparts dress conservatively. Bare shoulders are not acceptable, and short skirts are strictly for the young. Trousers and trouser suits are very popular among Korean women, and a well-tailored pair of trousers will prove suitable dress for most occasions.

Foreigners do not have to conform exactly to Korean standards, of course, but for those doing business in Korea, it is wise not to get out of line with Korean practice. Colourful sports shirts and shorts are not recommended for the office, even in the hottest and stickiest weather!

Wearing clothes appropriate for the occasion is seen as a mark of discernment. Koreans take leisure as seriously as work. If you are invited to play golf or tennis, therefore, it is important that you dress correctly. Even picnics and mountain-climbing demand the right outfit. No matter that you will be passed by numerous Koreans wearing quite the wrong shoes and clothes for mountain walks; the real gentleman (and lady) will have the right footwear, a proper hat and a stout stick. Again, Koreans will appreciate it if you have made the effort. In any case, such equipment makes sense when tackling the surprisingly rugged hills of Korea.

INTRODUCTIONS

When introduced, you should bend your upper body slightly. Koreans generally bow sparingly, unlike the Japanese. Amongst men, you should also offer your hand. There are no hard-and-fast rules about who should offer a hand first. If two Koreans meet, the senior will generally make the first move, but the same rules do not apply to foreigners. It is less common for Korean women to shake hands.

After the introduction, you should present your name card. Name cards are vital communication tools and are extensively used in Korea; it is a very good idea, therefore, to ensure that you have some with you even if you are only staying for a short while. You can, of course, have them printed at home but there are advantages in waiting until you arrive in Korea. They can be prepared quickly, and Korean printers will add your name, company or organization name and address in Korean.

Cards should be offered with both hands if possible, or, failing that, with the right hand. It is good form to study the card a little before putting it away. One useful purchase while in

Korea is a small wallet, usually leather or eel skin, in which to store both your cards and those which you have collected. Another good purchase is a card book to which you can transfer cards as your collection builds up.

Hot Tip: Avoid Eye Contact

Koreans tend to avoid too much eye contact, and consider it bad manners to look straight into another person's eyes all the time while conversing. Koreans fix their gaze between the eyes and the nose of the other person and will often glance downwards. Failure to 'look somebody in the eye' is not considered a sign of weakness in Korea. Neither is it necessary to provide a 'firm' handshake. Just a touch will do.

'Friendship' in *hangul* and Chinese characters

FRIENDS & FRIENDSHIP

Koreans rarely refer to somebody as 'friend' unless they know the person well. 'Friend' in Korean conveys the idea of what is signified by 'close friend' in English. Perhaps more than in the West, there is a distinction in Korea between friends and acquaintances.

In Korea, friendship involves obligations. Most Koreans, therefore, will have only a handful of friends, often acquired during school and college days or, among men, while doing national service. These friendships last. That said, it is certainly possible for a foreigner to make real friends in Korea and well worth the effort; but a deep level of commitment is expected, which may include what appears to be an encroachment on one's privacy and hospitality. For example, it is not unknown for a Korean friend to invite someone else to your house. This is not presumption on his part, but a feeling that the friendship with you is secure enough to permit such an extension of your hospitality.

KOREAN SURNAMES & GIVEN NAMES

The most common Korean surnames are Kim, Lee and Park, in that order. (You will also find the surname 'Lee' romanized as 'Rhee' and 'Yi', although in the Korean script it is spelt the same way.) As a result, millions of Koreans share the same surname, though they are not related. Families distinguish themselves by their place of origin, such as 'Andong'. Thus, you will find that the 'Andong Kims' are a family whose clan shrine is in Andong. Most surnames are one syllable, though there are a few two-syllable ones; 'Sa-Kong' is one example.

Given names are very important also in distinguishing people. Most Koreans have two-syllable given names. Frequently, one of the syllables will be shared by all the family members of that sex in one generation.

In the past, Koreans rarely used their given names. It is still regarded as impolite to use an adult's given name, and even Korean students will address each other by their surnames, or as brother and sister. The English terms, Mr, Mrs and Miss, have been adopted by Koreans and are used as frequently with surnames as are more traditional Korean forms of address.

Two of Korea's most common surnames

Hot Tip: Caution: Do Not Use Given Names

Koreans who have lived abroad, or who have spent a lot of time with foreigners, may be more relaxed about the use of given names, especially if they have adopted a Western name while abroad, which they can use when they are among foreigners. It is always sensible to check, however, that a Korean acquaintance is willing to be addressed by his or her given name in Korea.

Korean women, on the other hand, retain their own surnames after marriage. Do not be surprised, therefore, if Mr Kim introduces his wife as Mrs Park. Some Koreans who have spent a long time in the West may have assimilated the Western practice regarding a wife's name, but it is best not to assume that this is the case.

'Affection is not shown in public . . . except to small children'

Although younger Korean couples may now be seen holding hands in city streets, older Koreans generally tend not to show affection in public, except to small children. They will not be offended by foreigners exchanging a brief hug or kiss on greeting but will be surprised if this is repeated frequently.

You should also avoid expressions of displeasure. Displays of bad temper are regarded as the height of bad manners and are unlikely to achieve much. It is also best to avoid direct criticism as far as possible. If you have to criticize, do it in a vague and roundabout way, and do not do it in public. The direct approach will leave your audience embarrassed and uncooperative.

3

Food & Entertainment

'Traditionally . . . food is served all at once'

The staple food of Korea is short-grain rice (contrasting with Japan's long grain), although at times in the past it has been blended with other grains to stretch limited supplies. It is eaten from a ceramic or metal rice bowl with or without a lid.

Other tableware includes a soup bowl and various small and large plates for a variety of other food, often called side dishes. Food is eaten with a metal spoon and a pair of metal chopsticks. Sometimes you will be given wooden chopsticks in a restaurant. Unlike the Japanese and the Chinese, who use chopsticks for eating rice,

Koreans use a spoon. It is thought to be somewhat gauche to use chopsticks for rice. Try to master the use of chopsticks and spoon as a courtesy to your hosts and for your own convenience. In some restaurants, no other implements may be available. A knife in particular is considered a coarse object to bring to table. The food comes ready cut into bite-size pieces.

Koreans eat three full meals a day, with the number of dishes increasing at each meal. Traditionally, rice, soup and *kimchi* (see below) was served at all three meals, which meant that Korean housewives had to be up early to get everything ready. Nowadays, many younger Koreans in the cities have turned to Western-style cereals or toast as an alternative breakfast. Of course, Western-style food will be available in hotels, and even quite remote Korean hotels may serve some form of 'Western breakfast'.

Traditionally, food is not served in staged courses but all at once and eaten together. This was true in restaurants as well as private homes until recently. Before the 1986 Asian Games, the government decided that this was wasteful and not suitable for foreigners – who were not consulted – and decreed that all food should be served as separate courses, ordered individually. Gradually, however, the traditional way is creeping back. It is, in fact, easier for a foreigner to order a complete meal than to sort out the complexities of a Korean *à la carte* menu.

'Kisaeng party . . . similar to the geisha tradition'

You are not expected to consume everything that is put in front of you, but try as many dishes as you wish. Koreans consider it indelicate to lift the bowl of soup or rice to the lips as is done in China and Japan, or to use your hands to pick up food. In a traditional restaurant and in many homes, food will be served on low, individual, lacquered tables, with each diner having a complete meal on his or her table. Diners sit on cushions on the floor.

KOREAN CUISINE

The most famous of all Korean side dishes is probably *kimchi*. There are many forms of this dish, but the best known is made up of pickled cabbage seasoned with red pepper, garlic and ginger. Winter *kimchi* was made traditionally in the autumn to last the whole winter, and from November to March was often the only source of vitamin C. Winter *kimchi* is still made, even in urban households, although there are many other sources of vitamin C available. Its pungent taste and smell can be quite a shock.

In the summer, you will find mild 'water *kimchi*', usually made from cucumbers in a light brine. There are more than twenty regional variations of *kimchi*, each seasoned in different ways. Some caution is recommended when you first try it but most people come to like it. Foreigners find that some *kimchi* goes well with Western dishes; roast lamb seems to benefit from the strong flavour. *Kimchi* is such an important part of most Koreans' diet that you should not be surprised if it is served with Chinese and Japanese food in Korea.

'. . . you are not expected to consume everything'

Other popular dishes include *pulgogi*, or 'Korean barbecue', as it is sometimes known. Strips of beef are marinated in sesame oil, soy sauce, garlic, ginger and other condiments, and then cooked over a charcoal or gas brazier at the table. Short ribs, *kalbi*, are also popular and are cooked in the same way. Fish and seafood are also important elements of the Korean diet. As in Japan, raw fish, served with piquant seasonings, is highly regarded. Many styles of soup are served.

Two dishes, formerly exclusive to the royal court, now often appear at special banquets. The first is *kujolpan*, often called, somewhat poetically, 'nine-treasure dish'. This consists of small pancakes and eight special dishes, all presented in a nine-compartment lacquer dish. You select a pancake and one or more of the other dishes, wrap the latter in the former and away you go. The second is *sinsullo*, an individual hot-pot, with beef, vegetables and a variety of other ingredients all cooked over live coals. Very hot and very delicious!

Hot Tip: No Nose-blowing in Public, Please!

Koreans may slurp soup, burp after a meal, and clear their throats noisily, but they do not blow their noses in public. In general, be guided in such matters by how your fellow Koreans are behaving.

You are not obliged to burp if you do not wish to, still less to clear your throat as though you were trying to bring your shoes through your mouth! You will notice that Koreans who have colds will often wear a surgical mask over their mouths and noses.

EATING OUT

In a restaurant, you will often be brought a hot towel – cold in summer – to wipe your hands before the meal, and another at the end. Sometimes this will be in a plastic bag, sometimes not. Meals will usually end with plain fruit. You might be offered beer with your meal, or else a Korean tea. *Pori cha*, or barley tea, is particularly popular. It is served hot in winter and cold in summer.

The highest and most expensive form of restaurant entertaining is the *kisaeng* party, often, but not exclusively, held at a dedicated *kisaeng* house. The *kisaeng* tradition is similar to the *geisha* tradition in Japan. Both derive from the Confucian idea that it is the duty of women to serve men in all things. A typical *kisaeng* evening will involve large quantities of food and drink, with the *kisaeng* girls feeding their male companions and playing party games with them. There is also likely to be singing and dancing. In the past, the entertainment was confined to traditional-style performances by the *kisaeng*, but nowadays, the rest of the party are also likely to join in.

While it is not unknown for a foreigner to organize a *kisaeng* party, it is wise to be guided by a Korean before making any final commitments. 'Salons' or cocktail lounges will provide the female accompaniment in less exalted surroundings than the *kisaeng* house, but can also be expensive. 'Salons' may also be called 'business clubs', but the service is the same.

Hot Tip: Don't Pour Your Own Drink!

When drinking, you should not pour your own drinks. You should hold your glass in front of you, with both hands or with the right hand supported under the elbow by the left hand, and allow the host or somebody else to pour for you.

Similarly, you should offer to fill other people's glasses in the same way. If somebody toasts you, he will probably drain his glass. You should do the same, at least on the first occasion. It used to be the custom to exchange glasses for toasts but this is less common today for hygienic reasons.

Apart from Korean restaurants, there are a growing number of Western-style restaurants to be found in Korean cities. Most of these used to be located in the big hotels but this is no longer necessarily the case. All styles of food are available, from hamburgers to good French and Italian cooking. Seoul has had a Pakistani restaurant since the early 1980s, and now has a number of Indian restaurants. There are also many Chinese and Japanese restaurants, at prices to suit all pockets. Some are excellent.

You will by now have gathered that garlic forms an important part of the Korean diet. Garlic is indeed widely used, both on its own and as part of other dishes. Raw cloves of garlic will often appear as a side dish, or for adding to dishes such as *pulgogi* as they are cooking. There is no obligation to eat them, except on the principle of 'if you can't beat them, join them'. After a time, most people get used to the all-pervasive scent of garlic, and fail to notice it.

DOG SOUP

There has been much publicity in recent years about the eating of dogs and other 'strange foods' in Korea. Koreans do eat dog, usually in the form of a soup called *poshintang*, or 'body strengthening soup', but it is most unlikely that this would be offered to a foreigner, especially if not requested. The dogs used for cooking, Koreans are careful to point out, are not family pets, but are a species bred for the table. Dog restaurants and ones selling other exotic foods likely to be unfamiliar to foreigners were subject to strict regulation during the lead-up to the 1988 Olympics, but the controls have generally been relaxed since then. They do not, however, normally advertise their names in English and few foreigners are likely to be aware of their existence.

OTHER UNUSUAL DISHES

A refusal to eat these more unusual dishes, should they be offered, is unlikely to cause offence. Less likely to be offensive, but certainly unusual, are the numerous wild plants which Koreans eat. These include certain types of bracken, acorns made into a jelly, and bell-flower roots. They are often pickled, or served in a light brine, and most people find that they come to like them.

DRINKING IN KOREA

Koreans like drinking. Drinking parties, especially among men, are common and very popular. A few drinks shared in a bar with Korean acquaintances will go a long way towards friendship.

Koreans do not as a rule drink alone and they do not drink much without eating fairly substantial snacks called *anju*. This does not stop them getting drunk. There is no stigma attached to getting drunk in Korea, at least among men, and drinking parties may often become quite boisterous. Such sessions may be used to let off steam and to criticize the boss to his face, but without the dire consequences this might have in the West. The convention is that remarks made at drinking parties are not referred to the next day.

'. . . the two best known brands'

Beer is very popular in South Korea. There are several well-known Korean brands, including OB, Hite and Cass, and a number of variations, though most Korean beer is German-style lager. Foreign brands, usually brewed in Korea under licence, are also widely available in the big cities – but at a price. Heineken, Budweiser and Carlsberg are popular foreign brands. Some hotels offer even more exotic foreign beers, including both Guinness and British-style draft beer.

Western-style wine is made in South Korea. The white tends to be better than the red. French, Italian, American and Australian wines can be found in restaurants, and are often now on sale in hotel shops, in the big department stores, in supermarkets and in the growing number of convenience stores. In Seoul and some other cities there are specialist wine shops. Whisky and gin, both imported and locally produced, are widely available. Foreign brands are quite expensive, especially in hotels. Johnny Walker Black Label and Chivas Regal are particularly well-known brand-names among Koreans, and they make good presents.

Traditional Korean alcoholic drinks are every-where giving way to their Western competi-tors. They are worth sampling, however, if you get the chance. The most common ones are *soju*, the cheapest, generally the strongest and rather like vodka – though only about 25% alcohol by volume; *makkoli*, a milky-white drink, sometimes compared to beer, and now getting rarer; and *chongjong*, a rice wine, similar to Japanese *saké*, and like saké, served hot in winter and cold in summer. *Popchu*, a higher quality saké-like drink, is well worth seeking out.

In the past, Korean women did not drink until they were over 60. Today, it is not unusual for a Korean woman to take a glass of wine at a dinner, though most still only drink fruit juice. A few will drink quite a lot. But women rarely get drunk – it is bad form for them to do so – and a Western woman will need to take this into account. In any case, as already mentioned, a Western woman is unlikely to be invited to the more riotous parties. Although Korean men and women traditionally socialize mainly with their own sex, they generally understand Westerners' expectations of a mixed social gathering.

If you do not drink, do not worry. There are many Koreans who do not drink alcohol. Many 'Christians', by which Koreans understand 'Protestants', do not touch alcohol. It is also well understood that those taking certain medicines should avoid alcohol. More recently, random breath tests by the police are persuading more and more Koreans not to drink and drive. So if you wish to be excused, you can plead that you have religious convictions, that you are taking medication, or that you are driving.

Hot Tip: Singing is a Must!

If you do go out with a group of Koreans, you may
well find that as the evening progresses, your Korean
colleagues begin to sing. Before long, you too will
be called upon to sing.

When first asked, it is polite to decline. Indeed, it
is polite to decline more than once. But do not think
that you will escape! It is best to have a song or two
in readiness – however good or bad you are, there
will certainly be a demand for an encore.

'. . . before long, you too will be called on to sing'

When you leave a restaurant or bar, you will
not normally need to worry about the bill if
you have been invited by a Korean colleague. You
are the guest, and taking care of the bill is your
Korean host's responsibility. Koreans generally do
not like the Western custom of 'eating together

and paying separately'. The best way to repay hospitality is to invite your Korean friends to dinner after you have been entertained a couple of times. If you are in regular contact with a Korean colleague who visits your country, it may be simplest for you to offer entertainment on your home ground.

LEISURE & PLEASURE

A part from wining and dining, many other forms of entertainment are available in Seoul, and to a lesser extent in other cities. They are worth sampling.

Seoul has several concert halls. Western classical music enjoys great popularity in Korea, and a number of Korean musicians are acknowledged as world class. Concerts are often very good value for money. If you are going to hear a major international group, however, be prepared to pay high prices. Details of concerts can be found in the English-language newspapers or on the many posters which appear all over town. Ballet and Western opera are often available, and internationally acclaimed companies, such as the Royal Ballet, regularly visit South Korea. Western pop music is also popular. There are many Korean groups. Western performers are less frequent, partly because of tight control over the influx of some aspects of foreign culture.

Many Koreans enjoy the cinema, though as elsewhere, cinema-going is losing ground to television and home videos. In the past, political and cultural reasons led to restrictions on some Western films, but this is less common today. Western films shown in cinemas will usually be sub-titled; on television, however, they are generally dubbed. This can be entertaining for a short while, as the clean-jawed hero spouts impeccable Korean, but the novelty quickly wears off.

Visitors may find the English-language American Forces Korea Network (AFKN) TV pro-grammes more satisfactory. These include CNN and other news broadcasts, much sport, soap operas and the occasional film. Schedules for AFKN TV and radio are published in the English-language newspapers, which also list the Korean stations' programmes. There is also a Korean-organized English-language channel, called 'Arir-ang', aimed at foreigners in South Korea, but also broadcast internationally. Bigger hotels and a growing number of private homes have satellite TV, showing an increasing number of foreign-language channels.

The theatre is also thriving, and Western plays are regularly performed. It is said, for exam-ple, that in Seoul there is at least one Shakespeare play being performed somewhere every night of the year. The language barrier is again likely to prove too much for most visitors.

Of more interest to most visitors are perfor-mances of traditional Korean music and dance. Some traditional music may be rather strange on first acquaintance, but most people like the drumming and the dancing. Special performances for foreigners, often including a traditional meal as well, are put on at venues such as Korea House. These are often used by Korean organizations to entertain their guests.

Traditional dance and music

Another place to see traditional performances, and a good day out in its own right, is the Korean Folk Village south of Seoul, near the town of Suwon. This is very much in the style of European open-air museums. Buildings have been assembled from all over the Korean peninsula. As well as displaying the style of construction, the collection shows the difference between rich and poor and town and country. People dressed in traditional costumes run shops and workshops, making paper, pottery and other artefacts as their ancestors did. Authentic food and drink are available while you watch farmers' dances or other folk arts now rapidly disappearing from the countryside.

Visitors can also take advantage of regular lectures and tours organized by the Korea Branch of the Royal Asiatic Society, widely known to resident foreigners and Koreans as the RAS. Details can be found in the English-language press or direct from the RAS office in Seoul.

A visit to the 'truce village' of Panmunjom is an interesting, if somewhat chilling, experience. A further perspective on the Korean War can be found at the huge museum and memorial hall which makes up the 'War Memorial' complex at Yongsan in central Seoul. This also gives an account of Korean military history before and after the Korean War.

The major hotels will often have performances ranging from fashion shows to concerts. At the Sheraton Walker Hill Hotel in eastern Seoul, for example, Korean and Western performers offer Western-style cabaret. Rather more raucous floor shows can be found in various venues in Itaewon and other areas where foreigners gather, as well as in the fast-growing new entertainment areas south of the Han river. If you are venturing to such places for the first time, it is sensible to be guided by a knowledgeable foreign or Korean host.

Hot Tip: Golf is Good – But not Cheap!

The most common sport for the visitor is likely to be golf or tennis. Koreans are avid golfers, and there are many golf courses throughout the country. But be warned. It is very much a sport for the rich. If invited, and you play, you should accept in order to benefit from a further insight into Korean life that the occasion will provide.

As in other countries, much business is conducted in an informal way on the golf course. Tennis is less expensive.

Sport is very popular. Koreans have taken to baseball and soccer. Professional teams in both sports attract large crowds. It is occasionally possible to track down rugby games, but this is something of a minority sport. There is horse-racing in Seoul and a number of other cities.

Traditional Korean games of spinning tops and kicking shuttlecocks

SMOKING IN KOREA

Many Korean men smoke quite heavily, and although some restrictions are beginning to creep in, smoking is rarely prohibited in restaurants and other public places. Foreign brands of cigarettes are available, but are expensive. Younger Korean women rarely smoke, at least in public; but older ones, especially countrywomen, frequently do.

4

The Korean Home

'. . . ordinary life . . . conducted at floor level'

Koreans, unlike Chinese or Japanese, like to keep open house when friends are welcome any time. In rural areas, it is still customary to go 'house visiting' – visiting neighbours' houses after supper without prior arrangement. Instead of the living-room found in the West, rural Korean houses still have the *sarang bang*, or 'room for the guests', which is always open to visitors. Here people gather to talk, eat, drink and even to stay overnight. There is, therefore, a possibility that however short your visit to Korea, you may be invited to a Korean house.

Hot Tip: Rules of the House: No Shoes!

If you are invited to a Korean house, there are a few basic rules to follow. The first and most important is that shoes are not worn inside the house. This is true even if the house is Western-styled and carpeted. It is important, therefore, to take off your shoes in the entrance hall, before stepping into the house proper.

Much of ordinary life in a traditional Korean house is conducted at floor level. It is not just in restaurants that people eat their meals sitting on the floor. They do so at home as well. They also sleep on the floor. In these circumstances, it is very important that the floor is kept spotlessly clean; so shoes are left outside the living area. Remember also that it is not polite to show bare feet, so socks should be kept on. It is a good idea to make sure that they are clean. Nowadays, slippers may sometimes be provided for guests to wear inside the house, especially if it has carpets.

You will find that in other traditional-style buildings, such as temples and shrines, everybody removes their shoes. You should do the same. The advantage of wearing slip-on rather than lace-up shoes quickly becomes obvious. The need to keep floors spotlessly clean also explains why it is rare to see sandals worn without socks or stockings; feet will inevitably be dirty if sandals alone are worn.

UNDER-FLOOR HEATING

Traditional Korean houses used a system of under-floor heating called *ondol*. The hot gases from the kitchen fires were drawn under the floors of the living-rooms through a system of flues, thus providing heat. Today, especially in cities, the traditional *ondol* arrangements are likely to be provided by central-heating pipes running under the floor, but the principle is the same. You will find *ondol* rooms in hotels and restaurants as well as houses.

The *ondol* system provides great comfort on a cold winter's night. Should you, however, find yourself staying in a house or inn with the traditional type of *ondol* heating, it is wise to make sure that there is some form of ventilation; every year a few people are poisoned by leaking fumes in tightly closed rooms.

Koreans at home spend most of their time sitting on the floor. On the *ondol*, it is customary for men to sit cross-legged and for women to sit with their legs tucked under their bodies, or extended sideways, moving the weight slightly to one side. Stretching one's legs is considered impolite at all times. That said, most Koreans understand how difficult such postures are for Westerners, and a certain degree of latitude is allowed! You will also find that you will often be offered a backrest, rather like a legless armchair, to help make yourself comfortable.

THE KOREAN LOO

Most apartments and many houses in Seoul are equipped with Western-style toilets. However, rural houses, smaller restaurants and even some houses in Seoul and other cities will have squat-style toilets. You will usually find a pair of plastic sandals at the door of the toilet. You should put these on but remember that these are worn only in the toilet area. Toilet doors are usually kept closed, even when not occupied. It is wise to knock before entering; if the toilet is occupied, a discreet cough will tell you so.

Since the 1988 Seoul Olympics, the quality of public lavatories has improved immeasurably in Seoul in particular. They are also to be found at more frequent intervals than is usual in Asian cities. When travelling, and even in the less-frequented parts of Seoul and other large cities, it is as well to carry some paper tissues, since toilet paper is not always supplied. Sometimes, toilet tissue is sold from a vending machine just near the toilet block.

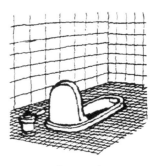

Squat style

Korean men tend to be strict about drawing a line between work and home. Most Korean wives, therefore, will know little about their husbands' business and would not expect to discuss it. There are exceptions, of course, especially among couples who have lived abroad. But on the whole, it is safest to stick to discussion of subjects such as children or family matters with most Korean wives.

Bedroom and *ondol* floor

If invited to a Korean home, you will find that the hostess probably does not join you for dinner. Even if there are servants, she will be busy preparing and supervising the food. She may join you at the end of the evening, but it is unlikely that she will eat with you. You should also be prepared for references to the lack of food suitable for guests. Do not worry! This is a standard politeness, not to be taken too seriously. Food in large quantities will appear.

5

Taboos

'. . . always take off your shoes in the entrance hall'

All countries have taboos and Korea is no exception. Traditionally, white clothes were worn for mourning, rather than black; but this was a special type of white cloth, off-white hemp, rarely seen except at funerals today. A white mourning band is still common, but a black band is also often worn nowadays for mourning purposes. You are in any case unlikely to be invited to a funeral but you might find yourself expected to pay respects if somebody of your acquaintance happens to die while you are in the country. Usually this involves no more than attending a memorial hall and solemnly bowing in front of a picture of the deceased.

Hot Tip: Beware of Number 4!

Koreans still avoid the number 4 (sa) since it has the same pronunciation as the word for death. Thus you will often find that Korean buildings do not have a fourth floor or you will find that the letter 'F' replaces the number 4. Because Koreans are aware of Western superstitions about the number 13, that too may be missing.

Another common taboo is against the use of the left hand to offer an object to somebody. It is best to offer something to another person, especially if they are senior in age or rank to you, with both hands. If that is not possible, use the right hand.

Do not touch a teenager or an adult on the head. The same prohibition does not apply to children, but on the whole it is best to err on the side of caution and avoid touching any Korean on the head.

Until recently, homosexuality was very rarely acknowledged in South Korea. Today its existence is more widely accepted, especially among university students. Yet you may still find Koreans who argue that it is something only known in the West. Nevertheless, do not assume that two boys or two girls walking hand in hand are homosexual. Walking thus, or with arms about each other's shoulders, is not a taboo in Korea, merely a sign of friendship. Conversely, a man and a woman who show too much affection in public attract disapproval.

There are today few formal restrictions on photography in South Korea. Some older people, especially in the countryside, may object to having their photograph taken, and it is best to avoid giving offence. As in many other countries, it is wise not to photograph anything that looks like a military installation or could be for military purposes. This may include airports.

Korean rice bowl and chopsticks

6

Shopping & Tipping

Traditional market, Seoul

Shopping in Korea is still great fun, especially in Seoul. Prices rose steeply at the time of the 1988 Olympics, which meant that there were fewer bargains available, but the 1997 financial crisis has again made Korean goods relatively cheap and the range on offer is still very wide. Whether it is Korean traditional products such as chests, ceramics, silk or ginseng, or more modern items such as electronic goods, cameras or clothes, there are still bargains to be found, especially if one is prepared to hunt further afield. Amethysts and smoky topaz are popular buys, as is Korean brassware.

There are a number of major shopping centres. They include traditional markets such as those around the South Gate (Namdaemun) and the East Gate (Tongdaemun), which are well worth a visit even if you do not intend to buy anything. Each carries a whole range of goods. There are also various smaller markets scattered about the city. Insa-dong, not far from the Kyongbok and Chang-dok Palaces, is the antiques' quarter of Seoul – it was known as Mary's Alley to an older generation of foreign residents. Prices today are very high. Less expensive is Itaewon, not far from the big US base at Yongsan.

Itaewon is a whole way of life for many foreigners in Seoul, who flock to its restaurants, hotels and bars. There is much night-life! By day, however, it is a good place to shop, with clothing stores in particular that are used to dealing with foreigners and can supply goods in foreign sizes. Over-eager sales staff can sometimes be off-putting, though a firm 'just looking' will usually ensure that you are left alone.

Most foreigners also enjoy shopping in the many underground arcades, which not only offer a wide range of outlets, but are relatively cool in the summer and warm in the winter. Itaewon and the arcades are home to many tailors who will make up suits and shirts quickly, though the day of the twenty-four-hour suit has long since passed. There are many department stores. Some of the longest-established are in the old downtown area around City Hall. Increasingly, these also have branches in the newer parts of the city south of the Han river. There are also many other retail outlets in these areas.

Cheap CDs and tapes can be found all over the city. Most are of reasonable quality. LPs, once widely available, are now rare. Foreign-language books can be bought at a number of places. The Kyobo Book Centre, a vast under-ground complex at the Kwanghwamun intersection midway between City Hall and the Kyongbok Palace, has a large foreign section. You can buy books in Chinese and Japanese as well as Western languages. It is also a good place to buy pens, pencils and other writing equipment. Another good bookshop in Seoul is at Ulchiro-1-ga subway station.

Several of the larger hotels have bookshops, and there are new outlets appearing regularly. The RAS has a good selection of books on Korea. There are several duty-free shops in Seoul, as well as duty-free outlets at Seoul international airport. These sell good-quality Korean products as well as the normal stock of such shops worldwide.

Hot Tip: The Good Tipping Guide

In theory, tipping is not required in most Korean establishments. There is no need to tip in a barber shop, a tea room or a bar. Taxi drivers do not expect to be tipped, though it is customary to leave the small change from a fare.

Porters at airports and stations should be tipped, in proportion to the number of bags they are asked to handle. Hostesses in 'room salons' and similar establishments are usually tipped, often quite heavily, but this is generally the responsibility of the host.

Big hotels add 10% to their bills and there is no need to leave anything further.

Few other Korean cities can match Seoul for the variety of shops and markets. But most big cities have one or two department stores, and there are duty-free shops in Pusan and Cheju. In smaller towns, local products can be a good buy. Chonju, the capital of North Cholla province, is famous for paper and paper products, for example. *Popchu* from Kyongju, already mentioned, is a superior type of rice wine.

You do not bargain over prices in the department stores or other big shops. In the markets and many of the arcade shops, it is fair to make an offer. Few goods will carry price tags. But remember that you are supposed to negotiate, not fight, with the shopkeeper. You will not find very much of English spoken except at the main department stores and in Itaewon. Shopkeepers get round the lack of a common language by

writing prices down or showing them on calcula-
tors. You can still bargain, by writing or punching
in, your suggestion.

Traditional hair-styles for women
Left: married; right: single

7

Gift-giving

Gift-giving is a very important part of Korean culture. As in Japan, gift-giving is often very formal, and is an integral part of most ceremonial occasions. As well as giving gifts on auspicious occasions such as weddings, birthdays and graduations, Koreans give gifts to mark various festivals and other events.

New Year and *chusok* (the harvest festival) gifts are particularly important. Other gifts are less tied to particular events. Students give gifts to their teachers; office staff to their bosses. A visiting foreigner on business will collect a surprising number of commemorative plaques, paperweights and other mementoes.

Although not essential, it can be useful to have a supply of company pens or other souvenirs to be able to give in return. If you are invited to a wedding or a similar important social landmark, it is as well to bring some form of gift. Remember that in Korea, it is perfectly acceptable to give money on such occasions. It should be suitably enclosed in an appropriate envelope, which should bear the name of the giver. Whatever you give, it will be welcomed as an indication of your understanding of Korean culture.

Gifts should be wrapped. If you cannot do this yourself, many shops will do it for you. In giving your gift, or in receiving gifts from others, a degree of diffidence is required. You should offer your own gift with suitable expressions of its unworthiness. Similarly, your Korean host will also play down the value of what is offered. Generally, if a gift is offered, you may make a modest show of refusing it once or twice, but if your host insists, you should then accept it. To really refuse a gift is insulting and shows a lack of proper understanding of Korean ways.

If invited to a Korean home, it is customary to take a gift. Gifts such as wine or whisky are much appreciated. As with other gifts, it is best to have them wrapped. Thus, whisky and other liquors are more acceptable if they are boxed, rather than just in the bottle. It is a good idea to bring items from home to give as gifts. Koreans are still relatively unfamiliar with internationally known brand-names, and so these are less important than a general air of good quality and good wrapping.

Hot Tip: Keep Your Present Wrapped!

Once accepted, you should not open the gift you have just received unless strongly pressed. Generally, Koreans will not press you to open their gift, and neither will they show much interest in opening your gift in your presence.

Good-quality jams and soaps are likely to be appreciated, as are books about your country. If you know that the people you are meeting have children, then a present for the children would not come amiss. Again, books are welcome, and collections of stamps are often appreciated. Presents for the children should supplement not replace those for the parents. One small gift often highly appreciated is copies of photographs taken during a visit.

Not all gifts are straightforward, especially in the business world. There may be occasions when a gift seems to be intended as a bribe, an offering designed to solicit favours. Such a gift will often be in the form of a white envelope containing money. If you have any doubt whatsoever, it is best to return the gift, without opening it, as soon as possible. Your action will be well understood.

8

Accommodation

Yogwan – 'tourist hotel'

You will find that South Korea is very well served for accommodation. In Seoul and the other major cities, there are many world-class hotels. They have all the facilities and the standard of service you would expect from such a type of hotel. In the big cities, they are good places to eat, to meet people and even to do some modest shopping. If you cannot manage without a particular Western brand of toothpaste, for example, there is a chance that you will find it in such a place.

If you wish to be more adventurous, then you should try some of the smaller and cheaper hotels. These are often described as 'tourist hotels'. They will have less in the way of facilities, but, especially away from Seoul, they will often offer good value for money. The staff will be less sophisticated than in the international-class hotels but will usually be helpful and certainly friendly.

Even more modest types of accommodation are *yogwan*. These are Korean inns. The Chinese characters read the same as the Japanese *ryokan*, but there are few Korean *yogwan* which equate to the *ryokan*. Only in the remoter islands or in some mountain areas is the visitor likely to come across a *yogwan* which is anything more than a concrete shell. But they can still be fun to stay in.

Remember that in most *yogwan*, the price includes at least dinner and breakfast – though do not be surprised if, away from the big cities, these two meals are more or less the same! Sleeping arrangements vary. In some you will find Western-style beds, in others you will sleep on the floor, Korean-style.

There is usually no rule about how many people stay in a Korean-style room. Just make it clear on checking in. Another thing to check is the standard of cleanliness. You will have no problems in the top-class establishments but the same standards may not apply in more remote areas. Do not hesitate to ask for a room to be cleaned, or for clean sheets and pillow cases, if you suspect that those offered you have been used before.

Quite apart from overnight accommodation, visitors may like to try two other traditional Korean experiences, the barber shop and the bath. Korean barber shops can be a very pleasant experience. You may not be able to appreciate the political and other gossip, but the combination of haircut, shave and massage that usually features in a Korean barber-shop's repertoire is quite an experience. It is as well, however, to stick to barber shops in hotels or other central locations. Sometimes other establishments can be a front for prostitution. As such, they are the target of frequent government campaigns against 'lewd practices'.

'Barber shops can be a very pleasant experience'

Hot Tip: Wash Outside the Bath!

Korean public baths, though now segregated, are friendly places, where inhibitions quickly disappear. As in Japan, you must soap and rinse yourself thoroughly in the public washing area before entering the main bath. Many baths are equipped with sauna facilities and resting rooms.

Korean public baths are similar to those found in Japan, with large communal bath-tubs. Where they survive, they will now often offer specialized pools. As South Korea becomes wealthier, they are being supplanted by similar, but more expensive, 'saunas', often in the bigger hotels.

The communal bath-tub

9

North Korea

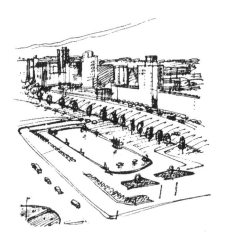

Pyongyang city centre

Until recently, the most that foreign visitors to the Korean peninsula saw of North Korea was on a trip from Seoul to the Demilitarized Zone (DMZ) at Panmunjom where the truce which ended the Korean War was signed in 1953. Such visits are still possible. But more people are now managing to visit North Korea. Although a number of guidebooks are now available covering North Korea, it is still relatively difficult to gain accurate information. In these circumstances, the following brief notes may be helpful for the first-time visitor.

The division of the peninsula in 1945 by Soviet and US forces, to effect the surrender of the Japanese troops which then occupied Korea, led in due course to the establishment of separate governments in the north and the south. While that in the south eventually developed along Western, free-market lines, North Korea, or the Democratic People's Republic of Korea, to give it its proper title, became a hard-line Communist state. Although sometimes described as 'Stalinist', in practice North Korea followed a line of its own, increasingly based on the ideas of Kim Il Sung, its first and only leader until his death in July 1994.

Kim Il Sung was succeeded by his son, Kim Jong Il, who is committed to following the path laid down by his father. The death of Kim Il Sung and the passing of real power to his son has led to much speculation about the possibility of dramatic changes in North Korea, and about an early re-unification of the peninsula. In the long run, reunification seems inevitable, given the long historical tradition of unity and the racial and cultural homogeneity of the Korean people. For the present, however, North Korea seems here to stay, even if some features of its political structure are being modified under the younger Kim. The most important development since 1994 was the agreement reached in April 2000 for a summit meeting between the leaders of North and South Korea, and the subsequent meeting in June 2000.

The two leaders, Kim Jong Il and Kim Dae Jung, seemed to establish a personal relationship, which may cut through the many problems of the peninsula.

As might be expected, visiting North Korea is quite different from visiting the South. In some ways, the visitor will find that the same standards of hospitality apply. Much effort will be devoted to making your stay a memorable event. But the North Korean attitude towards visitors reflects the very different political and social structure which operates in the North.

Statue of Kim Il Sung

There is no concept of independent travel in North Korea. Although in recent years there has been a greater willingness to receive visitors than was the case before the mid-1980s, such visitors will generally be tightly controlled. Most will come as part of a group, but even individual visitors with business to conduct will be handled as though they were part of some form of a package tour.

Since 1998, it has been possible for South Koreans to visit the Kumgang or Diamond Mountains, in tours organized by the South Korean Hyundai group, and these have now (early 2000) been opened up to some foreigners. The groups continue to be very tightly controlled, with no contact with the local people.

Although tourists can and do ask for a variety of programmes, all visitors find themselves on one or other of a set number of tours. These are made up of visits to Pyongyang, Nampo, the Myohyang Mountains, Haeju, Mount Paektu, Wonsan, the Kumgang Mountains, Hamhung and Kaesong. Visits to Kaesong are also likely to include a visit to the truce village at Panmunjom.

Occasionally, travellers with particular business to conduct may be able to go beyond these areas, especially to the new 'special economic zone' in the Najin-Songbon area in the far northeast of the country. On the whole, such excursions are still rare.

Hot Tip: Strict Control in North Korea

Both tour groups and individual travellers will find themselves strictly controlled. They will probably be watched carefully by their guides. Attempts to deviate from the prescribed route or to make contact with individual North Koreans are likely to be severely frowned upon.

Most visitors arrive by air, either through Russia, or, more usually, via Beijing. Occasionally, charter flights are available from Japan or Hong Kong. Those on the Kumgang tours arrive by boat. Visas are required. They can be obtained from a number of North Korean embassies in Europe, or from the North Korean embassy in Beijing. This is by far the most common way of getting a visa. Some travellers arrive by train from China. Customs formalities are in theory very strict, but providing one is not carrying material from South Korea, bibles or anti-Communist material, there should be no difficulty.

Although in theory there is no problem about visiting both North and South Korea using the same passport, many people find it more convenient to have two passports, to avoid confrontation. Another point to remember is that at present few Western countries have diplomatic or consular representation in North Korea. This might cause complications should a visitor get into difficulties. One other hazard of which intending visitors should be aware is that travel arrangements, even when made well in advance, may suddenly be cancelled with no reason given. In recent years, energy shortages have affected train schedules, especially in the winter months.

Visitors to North Korea stay in officially assigned hotels. These, in theory, vary in standard from deluxe down to third class, but those used by most Westerners will generally be of international standards, and prices. All meals are usually included in the price of the package tour. Food in general will be Korean, although there are some restaurants in Pyongyang which serve Chinese and Japanese meals. Breakfast will be vaguely Western-style. The casual visitor who has been to South Korea will probably not notice a great difference in styles of food.

Cold noodles

One great speciality in North Korea is cold noodles. These can be eaten in the South, but the original dish came from the North. Worth trying, even if only to provide a talking point on your next visit to the South. As well as Korean drinks similar to those described under the South Korean section, visitors will usually find beer readily available. It will be either locally produced or Japanese-made. In Pyongyang in particular, Western spirits can be bought in many of the hotels or in special shops which take hard currency.

There is no night life as it is popularly conceived. In Pyongyang, but not in other cities, the hotel bars serve as a meeting place for the small foreign community and for a small number of the North Korean élite. As well as drinks, such places will now often provide karaoke facilities. You are likely to be taken to some form of cultural manifestation. There are regular performances of revolutionary operas dealing with the heroic exploits of Korean guerrilla fighters during the struggle against Japan. These are spectacular displays of colour and music, more like Chinese 'opera' than opera as it is understood in the West. There is also a state circus and sporting performances. A golf course, for visiting foreigners, has been opened near Pyongyang.

There are few opportunities for visiting individual homes in North Korea. 'Home visits' do take place but these are far more formal than anything to be found in the South. In such circumstances, some small gift may be appropriate, but nothing lavish need be considered.

Until recently gifts were not required in North Korea. However, the increase in visitors, and the economic problems of recent years, seem to have brought about a change. Officials now appear to expect gifts such as whisky or cigarettes. If you do not wish to carry these, they can be bought in the hard currency shops. It is also sensible to have a small collection of pens and similar objects to give to guides or others who have proved helpful. Stamps may also be an acceptable present for a guide or other contact. Do not be surprised, however, if all such offerings are still refused away from Pyongyang.

As a rule, it is safer to avoid attempts at political discussion or probing about the political situation in the country. At best, such issues will be avoided and the attempt to raise them may cause offence. Visitors are likely to be asked to lay wreaths at the statue of Kim Il Sung or at some of the revolutionary sites associated with him. Those asked will need to decide for themselves whether they wish to do this. If they accept, there is a risk that such actions may be used for propaganda purposes. If they refuse, their guides are likely to express disappointment but not to insist.

Hot Tip: Only 'Sensible' Photographs!

Photography is permitted, but it is sensible to take precautions. Anything to do with the military or military installations is strictly taboo. This includes airports and aircraft. You may also find that your guides react in hostile fashion at any attempt to photograph things which show North Korea in a bad light.

Pyongyang's smart female traffic police are not keen on being photographed!

Your visit to North Korea may arouse interest and questions among your South Korean friends anxious to satisfy their curiosity. Even though it is now much easier for them to learn about North Korea than it was just a few years ago, and an increasing number have been able to visit the North, many South Koreans like to hear first-hand accounts. You will often find that many South Koreans will eventually reveal a family connection with the North, or even details of a divided family, as an explanation for their interest.

10

Useful Words & Phrases

The most widely used system of romanization in Korea is the McCune-Reischauer system, devised in the 1930s. A modified form of this is now used for most official maps and other publications, but you will occasionally encounter the 'Ministry of Education' system, which was used in the 1970s, and which is still sometimes found on maps and signposts. Here are some examples of how these two systems differ:

McCUNE-REISCHAUER: MINISTRY:
Soul   Seoul
Pusan   Busan
Kwangju   Gwangju
Cheju   Jeju

At the time of going to press, yet another system, similar to the Ministry of Education one, is being introduced.

Although written Korean is difficult, spoken Korean is easy and fun to learn. The following is a selection of useful words and phrases most often needed by foreign visitors:

NUMERALS

1: *Il*   20: *Ee-sip*

2: Ee
3: Sam
4: Sa
5: O
6: Yuk
7: Chil
8: Pal
9: Ku
10: Sip

30: Sam-sip
100: Paek
200: Ee-paek
300: Sam-paek
1,000: Chon
2,000: Ee-chon
3,000: Sam-chon
10,000 Man

GREETINGS

Hi! How are you? Good morning Good afternoon, Good evening	Annyong haseyo
Excuse me	Sille namnida
I am sorry	Mian hamnida
Thank you	Kamsa hamnida
You are welcome	Chon maneyo
Goodbye, so long	To mannap sida
I beg your pardon?	Ye? or Tasi malsamhae chuseyo

FOOD AND BEVERAGES:

Western food	Soyang eumsik
Korean food	Hankuk eumsik
Restaurant	Sikdang
Bar	Suljip
Tea house	Tabang
Liquor	Sul
Water	Mul
This is delicious	Aju masi sumnida
I'm hungry	Pae kopayo
I'm full up	Pae puloyo

SIMPLE PHRASES:

My name is. . .	Nae irum un. . .imnida
What is your name?	Irumi muosimnika?
What is that?	Jogosi muosimnika?
Where is. . .?	Odi issumnika?
This is good	Cho sumnida
How much is it?	Olma imnika?

Do you have. . .?	. . . issumnika?
Let's go to. . .	Kapsida
Please give me this	Ikot juseyo
What is it?	Ikosun muossimnika?
Right here, Please stop here	Yoki sewo chuseyo
Yes/No	Ye/Anio
Where is the restroom?	Hwajangsil odi issumnika?

PLACES:

Airport	Konghang
Seoul station	Seoul yok
Restroom	Hwajangsil
Subway	Chihachol
Bank	Unhaeng
Exit	Chulku
Entrance	Ipku
Store	Sangchom
Police station	Kyongchalso
Inn	Yogwan
Telephone booth	Kongjung chonwha
Post office	Uchekuk

The Korean Alphabet

Vowels ㅏ ㅑ ㅓ ㅕ ㅗ ㅛ ㅜ ㅠ ㅡ ㅣ

a　ya　ŏ　yŏ　o　yo　u　yu　ŭ　i

Consonants ㄱ ㄴ ㄷ ㄹ ㅁ ㅂ ㅅ

k, g　n　t, d　r, l　m　p, b　s, sh

ㅇ ㅈ ㅊ ㅋ ㅌ ㅍ ㅎ

ch, j　ch' k'　k'　t'　p'　h

안녕하세요 (How do you do?)

an　nyŏng　ha　se　yo

Further Reading

Lee Ki-Baik, *A New History of Korea*, translated by Edward Willet Wagner, with Edward J. Schultz. (Cambridge, Mass; London: Harvard University Press, 1984)

Hoare, James E. and Pares, Susan, *Conflict in Korea: an Encyclopaedia*. (Santa Barbara, CA, Denver, CO and Oxford, England: ABC-CLIO, 1999)

Leuras, Leonard and Chung, Nedra, eds, *Insight Guides: Korea*, updated by Bruce Cheeseman and Mike Breen. (Hong Kong: APA Publications, 7th edition, 1997)

Portal, Jane, *Korea: Art and Archaeology*. (London: British Museum Press, 2000)

Pratt, Keith and Rutt, Richard, *Korea: A Historical and Cultural Dictionary*. (Richmond, Surrey: Curzon Press, 1999)

Cumings, Bruce, *Korea's Place In The Sun: A Modern History*. (New York; London: W. W. Norton & Company Ltd., 1997)

Crowder Han, Suzanne, *Notes on Things Korean*. (Seoul and Elizabeth, NJ: Hollym, 1996)

Macdonald, Donald Stone, *The Koreans: Contemporary Politics and Society*, (Boulder, CO: Westview Press, 3rd edition, 1996)

Breen, Michael, *The Koreans: Who They Are, What They Want, Where Their Future Lies*. (London: Orion Business Books, 1998)

Oberdorfer, Don, *The Two Koreas: A Contemporary History*. (London: Little, Brown and Co., 1998)

Korean Words Used in This Book

Sinsullo 35	Hotpot
Soju 40	Alcoholic drink
Tongdaemun 59	East Gate
Yogwan 66	Korean inn

The ROK's national flag

ROK National Anthem

Andante maetoso (Refrain)

Music: Ahn Eak-tae

Dong Hae Mul Gwa Paek Tu San I   Ma Rŭ Go Dal   T'o   Rok

Ha Nŭ Nim I   Bo   U — Ha Sa   U   Ri Na Ra Man Se

(Refrain)

Mu — Gung Hwa   Sam — Ch'ŏl Li   HwaryŏGang —   San

Dae Han Sa Ram Dae Han — U Ro   Ki   Ri Bo Chŏn Ha   Se.

1. Until the East Sea's waves are dry, (and) Mt. Paektusan worn away,
   God watch o'er our land forever! Our Korea manse!

   Refrain:
   Rose of Sharon, thousand miles of range and river land!
   Guarded by her people, ever may Korea stand!

2. Like that Mt. Namsan armoured pine, standing on duty still,
   wind or frost, unchanging ever, be our resolute will.

3. In autumn's, arching evening sky, crystal, and cloudless blue,
   Be the radiant moon our spirit, steadfast, single, and true.

4. With such a will, (and) such a spirit, loyally, heart and hand,
   Let us love, come grief, come gladness, this, our beloved land!

Courtesy: Korean Overseas Culture & Information service

Facts About Korea

Land Area

The Korean peninsula is about 1,000 km (620 miles) long, with a total coastline of 17,361 km (11,000 miles). The average width of the peninsula is about 250 km (170 miles). There are over 3,500 islands.

North Korea: 120,540 sq. km
South Korea: 98,480 sq. km

Population

North Korea: 21,234,400
South Korea: 46,416,800

Language

The Korean language belongs to the Ural-Altaic group. It is thus related to Turkish, Finnish, Hungarian, Mongolian and Japanese. Both North and South Korea use the native Korean alphabet *hangul* to write the language. In South Korea, a small number of Chinese characters are also used, but this is no longer so in the North. Both Koreas enjoy very high rates of literacy.

Climate

Temperate, with four distinct seasons, and rainfall concentrated in summer. Summers are hot and humid, while winters are dry and cold. Temperatures range from -15°C in winter to 35°C in summer.

Currency

North Korea 100 *chon* = 1 *won*.
South Korea no longer has any smaller denomination than
the *won*.

The North and South Korean *won* have different values.
Credit cards can be widely used in South Korea. In North
Korea, their use is limited to the big hotels. In both
countries, US dollars and Japanese yen are widely
recognized and readily exchanged. You can change other
currencies at banks and at major hotels.

Electricity

North Korea: 220 volt 60 cycle. Visitors should note that
because of energy shortages, power cuts are frequent, even
in Pyongyang.

South Korea: Both 110 volt 50 cycle and 220-240 volt 60
cycle outlets are found. Hotels in big cities will probably be the
latter, but it is wise to check.

Transportation

North Korea has a very limited transportation system. The
railways suffer from the energy shortage. Rolling stock is often
very dilapidated. There appears to be little internal air travel
available to visitors. Most foreigners will go by road. Road
conditions range from fair to very poor.

The absence of traffic tends to encourage North Korean
drivers to go very fast, though the condition of the roads
outside Pyongyang makes this hazardous. Pyongyang has a
subway system, and an extensive network of buses and
trolleybuses. The buses and the trolleybuses are very crowded
and all suffer from periodic electricity cuts.

South Korea has a well-developed transport system, including an extensive domestic air network. There is a limited rail
network, but where it exists, it is well worth using. There are
good roads, including several expressways, and an extensive

system of long-distance buses.

Since the mid-1980s, the growth of car ownership has led to severe congestion on expressways and in the cities, especially at weekends and holiday periods.

There are ferry services to the main islands, including Cheju and Ullong. International ferries are available between Japan and China and South Korea. There is a growing subway network in Seoul, which is clean and efficient. Pusan also has a subway system.

Visas

For North Korean visas, see above.
Most Western visitors to South Korea do not require a visa for short visits. A valid passport is required.

Some Other Facts

Some ten million South Koreans, about one quarter of the population, call themselves Christians.

Korean celadon pottery is considered to be among the finest in the world.

The Korean language belongs to the Ural-Altaic group. It is related to Turkish, Finnish, Hungarian, Mongolian and Japanese.

Seoul, the capital of the Republic of Korea, celebrated the 600th anniversary of its founding in 1994.

Under the Korean system of reckoning age, a child is one year old on the day of its birth.

The first metal-clad ships were developed in Korea in the sixteenth century, and were used by Admiral Yi Sun-sin to defeat a Japanese fleet.

Index

This book originally appeared in 1988 as *Simple Etiquette in Korea*, published by Paul Norbury Publications. Since then, it has been extensively revised and enlarged twice by James Hoare and Susan Pares who are most grateful to the original authors, O. Young Lee and Seong-Kon Kim.